A SURPRISE BOOK

TOO BIG!

Michele Coxon

Happy Cat Books

For Luke Bailey, my computer whiz-kid
nephew, with love

Text and illustrations copyright © Michele Coxon, 2000

The moral right of the author/illustrator has been asserted

First published 2000 by Happy Cat Books,
Bradfield, Essex CO11 2UT

A CIP catalogue record for this book is available
from the British Library

ISBN 1 899248 69 2 Paperback
ISBN 1 899248 64 1 Hardback

Manufactured in China

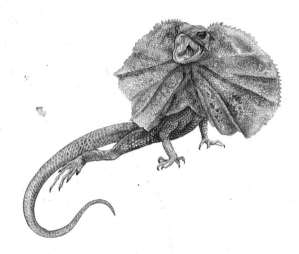

Other Lift-the-Flap Books by Michele Coxon

Catch Up, Little Cheetah!

Kitten Finds a Home

Look Out, Lion Cub!

Where's My Kitten?

Mother Wallaby is tired.

"You're a big girl now."
"I can almost squeeze in,"
squeaks Wallaby.

"No, out you get" says Mother. "I want someone to carry me!" calls Wallaby.

"Please carry
me, Koala!"

"Can I come in, Wombat?"

"Look after me, Emu!"

"Do you have a pouch, Kookaburra?"

"Perhaps I could live in your nest, Platypus?"

"Hello up there! Will you carry me, Possum?"

"I won't cuddle up to you,
Echidna."

"Your burrow looks cosy, Dingo."

"What a long scaly tail!"

"Oh mother, I am
pleased to see you!"

Wallaby feels very grown-up after her adventures. She and her new baby brother snuggle up close to their mother.